THE HANDBOOK

FOR

IRISH VOLUNTEERS

SIMPLE LECTURES ON MILITARY SUBJECTS

By " H "

The Handbook For Irish Volunteers
by "H"
Copyright © 2009 by the Caravat Press
Printed in the United States of America
Published by
Caravat Press
Philadelphia, PA

PREFACE

HAVING had many years experience as an officer, and having made a special study of drilling and thoroughly training the men under me, I am of opinion that I should place my experience and knowledge at the service of my fellow countrymen, who are engaged in the great Volunteer movement.

It is to help those who are animated with the truly patriotic spirit that dominates this movement that these lectures are written, so that when the day of trial comes we may stand shoulder to shoulder a calm, well disciplined army, hoping for peace, but prepared for war.

"H"

ORDER OF LECTURES

THE HANDBOOK
FOR IRISH VOLUNTEERS

CARE OF ARMS

1. Cleaning.—Great care must be taken of the **rifle.** It must be **cleaned daily,** all parts being wiped over with an oily rag, and the bore cleaned out with a piece of oily flannelette.

2. Special attention should be paid to keeping the bolt head free from rust, the striker way from becoming clogged, the aperture sights free from dirt.

3. The **magazine** must be always cleaned with a dry rag, as, if oiled, grit would collect and clog the action of the spring.

4. The Bore.—Having oiled the gauze of the pull-through, drop the weight through the breach ; never through the muzzle, for this would draw the dirt into the body ; pull it straight through three or four times. If the gauze becomes loose, pack the sides with narrow pieces of paper or flannelette. When the dirt softens, place a piece of flannelette in the loop next the gauze, and keep drawing it through and changing the flannelette until the latter comes out quite clean. Then pass a clean piece of oiled flannelette through the bore, which should be left thoroughly oiled, but not so that oil will trickle down into the body.

5. Make sure the pull-through is free from grit, and in drawing it through the barrel, don't let the cord touch the sides, or the friction of the cord may wear a groove in the barrel. This can easily be avoided if two men clean a rifle together, one holding it and the other pulling the cord straight through.

6. Cleaning after firing.—After firing, the rifle must be immediately cleaned, or if this is impossible an oily rag should be passed through the bore. The rifle must be constantly cleaned as long as any cordite shows in the barrel. Only the regulation flannelette and mineral jelly should be used for cleaning the bore of the rifle.

7. The size of the flannelette is never to exceed four inches by two inches, but can often be reduced with advantage when using an oily rag. Oil should be well shaken before it is used.

8. Cartridges must not be left in the magazine except when actually necessary. It weakens the spring.

9. When you have finished cleaning your rifle, see that the trigger is pressed and the safety catch is back at safety.

Questions on Lecture

1. How often do you clean your rifle ?
2. How do you clean it, and what parts require special attention ?
3. How do you clean the magazine ?
4. Describe how you would clean the bore ?
5. What must you guard against when cleaning the bore ?

6. If you are unable to clean your rifle immediately after firing, what should you do ?

7. What size flannelette will you use ?

8. How many cartridges do you keep in your magazine ?

9. Having finished cleaning your rifle, what is the last thing you should see to ?

AIMING

1. Aim : where taken.—Aim should be taken at the lowest portion of the object.

2. Because :—

    (a) In overestimation you may hit the enemy in the head.

    (b) If you underestimate the distance, you may catch him with a ricochet.

    (c) A late shot may get home at a vanishing target.

    (d) In excitement and at night men shoot high.

    (e) Generally the most vulnerable part.

    (f) It helps to find the range.

If you fire at the head of a man standing up, and the bullet just misses his head, it may not strike the ground for another 200 yards, and you will promptly come to the conclusion that you have over-estimated the distance by about 200 yards. You bring down your sights, and the next shot is short. Now you don't know at what range to fire. If in the first instance you had aimed low, about the man's stomach, you would know you had missed him, but the bullet striking the ground much closer to him would show that the range was about right. The next time, aiming more carefully, you would probably hit him.

(g) The rifle is so sighted that if you aim at the bottom of a target you will hit the centre.

3. The Three Rules for Aiming are :—

1. See that your sights are upright.
2. That the tip of the foresight is seen in line with and in the centre of the shoulders of the notch of the back sight.
3. Then carry your sights to " six o'clock " on the object.

4. Target Indication.—In order that any particular part of a target can be pointed out easily and quickly, imagine the target represents the face of a clock. For example take a bullseye target. The highest point of the bullseye will be twelve o'clock, the lowest point or bottom of the bullseye six o'clock. Half way on the right, between twelve and six o'clock will be three o'clock and half way on the left nine o'clock, you can thus represent any part of the bullseye by an hour. So when told to carry your sights to six o'clock on the bullseye you know you are to carry them to the lowest part.

5. Six o'clock line.—The six o'clock line is an imaginary straight line drawn under but touching the object aimed at. For example, in firing at men who have taken cover behind a wall and are firing over it, the top of the wall would represent the six o'clock line. Firing at men crossing the sky line, the sky line would represent the six o'clock line.

6. Correcting Elevation.—When firing, if your shots tend to go high, lower your sights a little ; if, on the other hand, they go low, raise them, but never vary the amount of foresight, or aim off the six o'clock line.

7. Wind.—The bullet is very much affected by currents of air. A following wind tends to make it go high. A head wind to go low. A side wind to push it to the side.

8. In aiming, it is necessary, therefore, to allow for wind ; and for military purposes wind is measured in feet. For example, a man is asked the strength of the wind. He replies one foot of right wind, by which he means that to hit the target he intends to aim one foot to the right of six o'clock on the target. Therefore, allowance for a side wind is made by aiming off the target into the wind, but never off the six o'clock line.

Take an example : Suppose you want to allow for one foot of right wind. First take aim as if there was no wind blowing ; then along the six o'clock line carry your sights one foot to the right. The greatest care must be taken in doing so not to bring your rifle above or below the six o'clock line.

If a left wind was blowing, you would do the reverse.

For a head wind raise your sights.

For a following wind, lower your sights.

9. Sight.—(a) Lights high, sights high.
        (b) Lights low, sights low.

Bright light shining on the sights makes it difficult to judge when correct sighting has been taken. The foresight appears too clear and bright and the amount required is under-estimated. Shots tend to go low and sights must be raised. Therefore lights high, sights high.

10. In dull or misty weather, the foresight is more difficult to see, too much is taken. Shots tend to go high, lower sights. This also occurs in shooting in the early morning, at dusk or by night, in fact whenever there is a bad light.

11. Aiming at moving objects.—To hit an object moving across your front, aim will first be taken in the ordinary way, and then carried sideways in advance of the object as if allowing for wind. The amount depends on the rate of movement of the object.

12. Roughly up to 500 yards :—*

Allow 1 ft. per 100 yards for a single man walking.

   ,,   2 ft. ,,   ,,   ,,   ,,   ,,   ,, doubling.

   ,,   3 ft. ,,   ,,   ,,   ,,   horseman trotting.

   ,,   4 ft. ,,   ,,   ,,   ,,   ,, galloping.

13. In firing at an object advancing or retiring, allowance must be made for the distance constantly changing by firing higher or lower. There is no time to alter sights. If the enemy is advancing, fire at the ground just in front ; if retiring, fire at his legs.

14. When firing at a column, aim should be taken at the head of the column.

Questions on Lecture

1. What part of an object would you aim at ?
2. Why do you aim at the lowest portion ?

* "Infantry Training."

3. What are the three rules for aiming ?

4. How would you indicate accurately a certain portion of a target ?

5. What is understood by the six o'clock line ?

0. When firing, suppose you noticed your bullets were striking the ground in front of the object, what would you do ?

7. What effect has wind on a bullet ?

8. How do you allow for wind ?

9. What effect has bright light on your shooting ?

10. What effect has dull light on your shooting ?

11. How would you aim at a man running across your front ?

12. Supposing he were 300 yards away, how far would you aim in front ?

13. How would you fire at a man running towards you ?

14. At what part of a column would you aim ?

FIRING EXERCISES

Positions used.—The positions used are the lying, kneeling, standing and sitting.

Lying.—Always lie down to fire, unless by doing so you lose sight of the object.

(a) You present a smaller mark to the enemy, which gives you confidence and steadies your aim.

(From figures prepared at the School of Musketry,

Hythe,* it appears that whether extended or not, men standing are from three to four times as vulnerable as when lying down, and men kneeling, twice as vulnerable as when lying. The difference is more marked at the shorter ranges.) To be vulnerable means that one can be wounded.

     (b) It is the most comfortable and accurate position for firing.

     (c) The nearer your rifle is to the ground, the lower will your bullet keep, and the better chance you have of hitting the object aimed at.

Kneeling.—Fire kneeling when you cannot see the object lying ; for example, firing over low walls, in meadows, over low hedges, etc.

Standing.—The standing position is used when the object cannot be seen kneeling, as in firing over high walls, in very long grass, rushes, etc. It is also very useful for imparting instruction in the rifle exercises. In long grass, or undulating country, men should not open fire in standing or kneeling positions unless required by the tactical situation. The cover should rather be used to get forward to a favourable fire position.

Sitting.—When firing down hill this position will be adopted. It is very difficult to locate a man sitting on the slope of a hill if the background is similar to his uniform. He does not show up. His movements, that is, loading and bringing the rifle to his shoulder, are almost imperceptible and by the report of his rifle alone can he be discovered.

---

* Lecture delivered on Fire Tactics at the School of Musketry, Hythe.

Common faults in position and the results :—

(1) *F.* Not facing the object and not keeping your eyes fixed on it while getting into position.

R. (*a*) Loss of time in aiming; your rifle will not be pointing straight at the object.

This is especially the case in the lying position, because as you lie down, oblique or crosswise to the line of fire, your rifle may be pointing more towards the next man's head than the object. It then requires much shuffling to get into position, once down badly it is hard to get comfortable, which means a man quickly tires if firing has to be sustained for any length of time.

(*b*) Loss of object.

A man drops down in long grass and finds he is unable to see over it. He ought to be kneeling.

(2) *F.* Failing to make the half turn.
R. Uncomfortable position.

(3) *F.* Loading position standing; small of the butt not far enough forward.
R. Difficulty in working the bolt, and also loss of time, when coming to the aiming position.

(4) *F.* Failure to draw back bolt to full extent.
R. A jam, and the loss of two rounds.

(5) *F.* Carelessness or slowness in adjusting sight.
R. Bad shooting.

(6) *F.* Shifting the grasp of the left hand when coming to the aiming position.
R. Loss of time in getting aim.

2

(7) *F.* Failure to grasp the small firmly, with the thumb and three fingers of the right hand.

R. Loss of power and a tendency to jerk trigger.

(8) *F.* Holding the rifle with the tips of the fingers, instead of firmly diagonally across the hand with the wrist kept well up.

R. Loss of time and power.

(9) *F.* Standing position, left elbow not well under the rifle.

R. Lack of support.

(10) *F.* Right elbow lowered below the level of the shoulder.

R. Sights inclined to the right, and there is a tendency to jerk the trigger The bullets will fall to the right, and low.

(11) *F.* Right elbow raised above the level of the shoulder.

R. Sights inclined to the left. The bullets will fall to the left and low.

(12) *F.* Eye too near the cocking piece.

R. Increase of blur and less accurate aim.

(13) *F.* Failure to restrain your breathing at the moment of pressing the trigger.

R. Unsteadiness.

(14) *F.* Inability to press trigger when the sights are on the object.

R. The trigger finger or first finger of your right hand has probably slipped up too high on the trigger. Have your rifle tested to see the pull off is not too strong.

(15) *F.* Careless position of the butt in shoulder or holding it there loosely.

R. Probable bruising of collar bone and consequent flinching when firing.

(16) *F.* Taking the eyes off the mark when loading.

R. Loss of time ; especially in rapid fire. A moving object may be completely lost to sight.

(17) *F.* Looking at sights last instead of the object aimed at.

R. The object is blurred and the shot goes wild.

To conclude I will quote an incident in the Battle of Sha-ho—Russo-Japanese War, from General Sir Ian Hamilton's book, " A Staff-Officer's Scrap Book " :—*

" The Okasaki Brigade was crossing the open to try and storm Terayama by one supreme effort ; and the only English expression which will convey any idea of their haste is that phase of the hunting field—' Hell for leather.'

" Bullets fell thick amongst those who ran for life or death across the plain, and the yellow dust of their impact on the plough rose in a cloud almost up to the men's knees. By what magic these bullets almost always struck in the vacant spaces and very rarely on the bodies of the men, I cannot explain, beyond saying that it is ever thus with the bullets of a bad shooting corps."

---

* By permission of the publisher, Mr. Edward Arnold.

COVER

1. General Remarks.—With the increase in the range and accuracy of modern firearms it has been found that troops advancing to an attack, unless they take advantage of both natural and artificial cover, cannot hope to penetrate the enemy's lines of defence.

2. Kinds of Cover.—In speaking of cover, one distinguishes between :—

    (1) Cover from view.
    (2) Cover from fire.

3. Cover from view implies anything that renders you invisible to the enemy.

4. Cover from fire implies something more solid, a ditch, a wall, a trench, something that the enemy's bullets cannot penetrate. It also implies cover from view, but with the important difference that if you are behind a rock or in a trench the enemy may know you are there, but as long as you stay there he cannot get at you. He will do his utmost to catch you as you come out. Whereas, with cover from view only, if he can locate your cover, a change of position will benefit your health. Notwithstanding this, cover from view possesses many advantages over cover from fire.

5. It is very easily found and very hard to locate.

Each man in a skirmishing line advancing to the attack must take what cover he can find to his front. Men cannot crowd right or left in search of it. Drop down in the grass or in a fold of the ground, keep your body still, and if you are wearing khaki uniform it will be hard to locate you.

Remember that it is necessary to see a man before you can shoot him. Bear this in mind and avoid all conspicuous cover such as single trees, rocks, etc. They only draw fire and probably the range is known to a nicety.

Before the battle of Mukden the Russians took all possible ranges to all prominent features and posted them up in the trenches, so that they might be known to all. The Japanese also paid great attention to cover from view, and seem to have regarded it as more essential than cover from fire. General Sir Ian Hamilton testifies to this in his book, "A Staff Officer's Scrap Book."* Writing of their preparations before the battle of the Yalu, which opened the campaign in Manchuria, he says :—

" Every advantage was taken of the natural lie of the ground, and much artifice was employed to conceal the position from the Russian gunners on the North bank of the river. Trees were transplanted a short distance in front of the batteries to hide the tell-tale flash of the discharge, and were carefully chosen from those either growing *directly* in front or *directly* behind the entrenchment to be concealed. The next morning the landscape appeared unchanged from the Russian side of the river, as the fact that a tree of a particular shape had advanced or retired two hundred or three hundred yards during the night was naturally imperceptible. Poles were stuck into the sand and connected by a string on which branches

---

* By permission of the publisher, Mr. Edward Arnold.

were suspended. The earth dug out of the deep gun pits was most carefully and with great labour scattered broad cast so as not to disclose any irregularity of terrain.* . . . numbers of covered ways leading down to the river showed the trouble that had been taken to ensure a plentiful supply of water for laying the dust, which is otherwise so apt to rise with the shock of discharge and give away the position. When all had been done that could be done to ensure concealment then all was done that could be done in time to ensure safety. After all, the first essential of hitting an enemy is to see him, and a captain of one of the Japanese howitzer batteries told me that throughout the artillery action of April 30th the Russians never had a notion of his whereabouts. Not a single missile of any description came within three hundred yards of the Japanese howitzers, whose shooting was carried out, therefore, as calmly as if they had been at a practice camp. It was equally good too. On one spot, fifteen yards by fourteen yards, where a Russian battery had been, I counted eight craters made by their high explosive shells."

Suit your body to the cover. If behind a wall get your feet in close. If behind a stone or the stump of a tree, don't adopt the correct firing position but lie straight behind it. Don't be an ostrich and think yourself safe because your head is out of sight. Some of us have large feet, they may be seen.

6. When Effective.—It is laid down in "Infantry Training," that "Cover to be effective must fulfil the following conditions :—

---

* Terrain means ground.

" 1. Afford a good view of the ground to the front
(If the volunteer is to shoot with effect he must
never lose sight of what he wants to fire at.)

" 2. Allow free use of the rifle.

" 3. Give concealment to the firer.

" 4. Provide protection against the enemy's fire."

Remember these, especially the first, which says, there
should be a good field of view to the front. It is no use
to sit in a ditch that you can't see over You would lose
touch with the enemy.

7. Cover for Defence.—Defensive cover when time per-
mits will usually take the form of trenches, and it is not
necessary now to explain the different kinds that may be
used, but they should at all times be provided with loop-
holes through which a steady stream of fire may be poured
by the defence at little risk to themselves. A trench
well provided with loop-holes does away with that unpleasant sensation of popping up to fire, such fire being
often badly delivered and therefore ineffectual. Writing
of the battle of Nanshan, General Sir Ian Hamilton says :—*

" I noticed an important advance on the Yalu defences.
The first line of trenches which followed the curve of the
hills about twenty-five feet above their base was com-
pleted with sand-bag loop-holes. It was owing to the
loop-holes and the barbed wire, that ten thousand Russians
resisted the third Army of forty-two thousand men and
the first Artillery Brigade until sunset, although their
Artillery had been completely silenced by 9 a.m."

---

* "A Staff-Officer's Scrap Book," by General Sir Ian Hamilton. By
permission of the publisher, Mr. Edward Arnold.

Questions on the Lecture

1. Why is it necessary to make use of cover ?
2. Name the different kinds of cover ?
3. What is meant by cover from view ?
4. What is meant by cover from fire ?
5. What advantages has cover from view over cover from fire ?
6. When is cover effective ?
7. What is essential in cover for defence ?

SKIRMISHING

Men are said to be skirmishing, when they move along in extended order, making use of all possible cover, their thoughts bent on accomplishing a common task. Their aim may be to surround an isolated farmhouse, to seize a hill, etc.

Skirmishing is the formation adopted by Infantry under fire.

1. The object of skirmishing is to enable the firing line to move forward without suffering heavy loss from the time they come under fire until they get within decisive range (about 600 yards) of the enemy.

In brief, the object of skirmishing is to enable the firing line to close with the enemy with as little loss as possible.

There are certain points to be remembered if you wish to become a good skirmisher :—

Exact obedience to the whistle.

2. The moment you hear the sound of the whistle, look

towards your leader and watch for his signal; obey it instantly.

It is laid down in " Infantry Training," Section 49, that:
" All movements of skirmishers will be controlled by the whistle and signal, for which purpose the following whistle blasts and signals have been adopted :—

3. Whistle Blasts.

The whistle will be used—

    (a) To draw attention to a signal about to be made—" a short blast."

    (b) To denote " Cease fire "—" A long drawn out blast."

    (c) To denote " Rally," in wood, bush, fog or darkness, when the signal cannot be seen —" a succession of short blasts."

    (d) To denote " Alarm "—" A succession of alternate long and short blasts."

On a short blast being blown on the whistle, skirmishers will turn towards their commander and will remain looking at him until he gives the executive signal.

4. Signals.

SIGNAL	TO INDICATE
(a) Arm swung from rear to front below the shoulder,	" Advance " or " Forward "
(b) Arm circled above the head,	" Retire "
(c) Hand raised in line with the shoulder, elbow bent,	" Quick time "
(d) Clenched hand moved up and down between thigh and shoulder.	" Double "

(e) Arm raised at full extent above head,   " Halt "

(f) Body or horse turned in the required direction and arm extended in line with the shoulder,   " Incline "

(g) Circular movement of the extended arm in line with the shoulder in the required direction,   " Wheel "

(h) Two or three slight movements of the open hand towards the ground,   " Lie down "

(i) Arm at full extent over head and waved a few times slowly from side to side, the hand to be open and to come down as low as the hips on both sides of the body,*   " Extend "

(k) Hand placed on the top of the head, the elbow to be square to the right or left, according to which hand is used,†   " Close "

(l) Arm swung from rear to front above the shoulder,   " Reinforce "

---

* This signal denotes extension from the centre. If the extension is to be made to the right, finish the signal by pointing to the right. If the extension is to be made to the left, finish the signal by pointing to the left.

† This signal denotes " Close on the centre." If it is desired to close on the right, finish the signal by pointing to the right. If the close is to be on the left, point to the left.

(m) Weapon held up above, and as if guarding the head, — " Enemy in sight in small numbers "

(n) As in (m), but weapon raised and lowered frequently, — " Enemy in sight in large numbers "

(o) Weapon held up at full extent of arm, point, or muzzle, uppermost, — " No enemy in sight "

(p) Weapon held up at full extent or arm, point, or muzzle, downwards — " Running short of ammunition "

Note.—All signals should be made with whichever arm will show most clearly what is meant.

Signals (m) (n) (o) (p) should be answered by repeating them.

The number of paces to which men are to extend is to be communicated by word of mouth.

5. War bugle calls.

War bugle calls—Charge, Alarm.

No other calls are to be used. For the Cease Fire the whistle only is to be used.

6. " Look before you leap," that is, before leaving your present cover, select another and straight to your front.

Advance straight to your front, otherwise crowding is bound to occur, which would give the enemy a chance for rapid fire, at a large target.

7. In getting from fire position to fire position, make long rushes, and simultaneous advances of long lines of men are best. Covering fire will be provided by the supports and reserves.

It is better to gain cover in dead ground to the right or left than to move over high ground exposed to the enemy's view, but don't lose direction, get back to your old line of advance as soon as possible.

8. Once behind cover, all unnecessary movements are to be avoided, especially by defenders of a concealed position. Don't roll over and wave your feet in the air, or when pushing forward your rifle don't let the muzzle be seen. A small thing may give away a position, as General Sir Ian Hamilton shows in writing about the retreat from Penlin in the Russo-Japanese War.

The Japanese Infantry attack had been held for a considerable time by the fire of the Russians from a sunken road. The Japanese Artillery could not locate this road. General Sir Ian Hamilton writes : *

" Attentively watching, the commander of the six little guns was at last enabled to locate the exact position of the intractable sunken road by a fortunate accident. A company of the enemy's Infantry inefficiently led, showed themselves on the crest line in close order, and on being scattered by shrapnel some of them were observed to step down and disappear entirely from view. . . . The Battery Commander now knew what to do ; and his fire, which had been so far at random and ineffectual, immediately became concentrated and deadly. Shrapnel whistled over the sunken road, and high explosive shells dropped into it, until in a very few minutes the musketry was dominated by the gun fire."

---

* " A Staff-Officers Scrap Book," by General Sir Ian Hamilton. By permission of the publisher, Mr. Edward Arnold.

Again writing of a small fight between a few companies of Russo-Japanese on the Mot'enling Pass, July 11th, 1904, he says :—

" The Russians had a considerable advantage in command even where they had taken up their alignment some distance down the wooded Northern spur of ' E.' This advantage was, however, much more than counterbalanced by the misguided spurious gallantry which impelled the Russian officers to stand up, not only exposing themselves unnecessarily but also disclosing the exact position of their sections, and thus drawing fire on their men."

9. As the instant of leaving cover is the most dangerous, be as quick as possible.

If the enemy see you drop behind a piece of cover, they will cover it with their rifles, and the moment you appear bang go the rifles. If you come out slowly you are sure to be hit, but spring out and the bullets will fall behind.

Know the quantity of various things required to make a cover bullet proof.

10. Generally speaking the drier and looser the material used, the less will be required to make the cover bullet proof, for loose material turns the bullet. About two and a half feet of sand, or three feet of loose earth free from stones will be sufficient. But rammed clay, like a clay ditch, would need to be four feet thick to be safe.

11. Only very large trees are bullet proof, and the penetration is much less *across* than *with* the grain.

An oak or a pine two and a half feet thick will give protection.

12. Skirmishers should always work in pairs. It gives

confidence. When one is firing, the other one can watch the effect and look out for movements of the enemy, correct the range, etc. When one advances the other gives him covering fire. It helps oblique or cross fire, which is the only way you can hit a man behind cover.

13. Things to be avoided.—There are certain things a skirmisher must avoid.

    1. *Crowding* behind cover even when bullet proof.

You may never be able to get out again. If the enemy know you are there, they will direct a hot fire all round the cover, making it almost impossible to get away in safety.

    2. The sky line.

An example has been quoted already of a position being given away by men appearing on the sky line.

    3. All unnecessary movements.

    4. Waste of ammunition.

Take care of your ammunition. Depend on covering fire as long as possible. It is extremely difficult to obtain fresh ammunition during an attack. Husband it for the close range ; for if you then run short you can do nothing and the attack must fail.

14. Skirmishers versus Cavalry.

    1. If they are trained cavalry, use your rifle as well as you can ; but *don't* form rallying squares, because they would make a target for artillery.

15. What to watch out for.

    1. Keep a fair line.

2. A chance of oblique or enfilade fire. Enfilade fire is fire delivered from a flank. For example, to enfilade a road means to fire straight up or down it.

To enfilade a trench, fire straight along it.

Enfilade fire is most deadly, because firing, for instance, along a trench occupied by the enemy, you ought to hit a man every time, and under- or over-estimating the range makes no difference.

3. Down with the enemy's leaders.

4. Fire at short range if you get the chance, but carefully or you are only wasting ammunition. It is astonishing how often men are missed at short range.

5. When things are mixed up, look out for the nearest leader and take his orders.

6. See that commands and instructions are carried out to the best of your ability.

7. Pass orders quickly and accurately.

In passing the range down a skirmishing line, pass it on at once, *before* you alter your own sights. Sometimes you see a man alter his sights and commence firing before he thinks of passing on the range. This causes unnecessary delay in the passing of the order.

Questions on the Lecture

1. What is the object of skirmishing ?

2. What must a skirmisher do on hearing a short whistle blast ?

3. Blow the whistle blasts used.

4. Make the signals used.

5. What War bugle-calls are used ?

6. Before advancing from behind cover, what must you do ?

7. How do you advance from cover to cover ?

8. What must defenders of a concealed position carefully avoid ?

9. Why, when advancing, is it necessary to spring out from behind cover ?

10. (a) Is rammed clay as bullet proof as loose clay ?

(b) How much of each will stop a bullet ?

11. (a) Can you count on trees being generally bullet-proof ?

(b) Will a bullet penetrate further with the grain than across the grain ?

12. Why ought skirmishers to work in pairs ?

13. What ought a volunteer to avoid when skirmishing ?

14. What ought skirmishers to do if attacked by cavalry ?

15. What ought a skirmisher to be on the watch for ?

JUDGING DISTANCE

1. General Remarks.—The more proficient a volunteer becomes in shooting, the greater is the necessity that he should be a good judge of distance.

A " Marksman," for service purposes, means the man who can fire the first effective shot at unknown range.

A " third class shot," for service purposes, means the man who gets hit by the first effective shot while he is thinking about the range.

As the estimation of the distance of an object depends on the clearness or dullness of the atmosphere, nature of the country, etc., it follows that the conditions will be changed in different countries, but somé general rules apply to all.

2. Methods for Judging Distance.—There are three methods for judging distance :—

    1. Measure the intervening ground with your eye.
    2. Judge the range from the impression given to the eye by the object.
    3. Combine both systems.

We will take these methods separately.

First Method.—The first, *i.e.*, " Measure the intervening ground with your eye."

Learn to recognise distances of one hundred yards in any variation of light, ground and background. When you have got this unit of measurement firmly fixed in your eye, try a longer distance. Try and count how many measurements of one hundred yards each there are between you and the object.

For example, a man is crossing your front and you want to discover how far he is away. You look at the intervening ground and think in your own mind, well ! 'tis one hundred yards to that bush, another to the tree, another to the house, that is three hundred yards, he is about fifty yards beyond, that is three hundred and fifty yards. Work it out in some way like that, but always

3

be able to give a reason why you think the distance is so and so. Never guess. Guessing is useless. Sometimes the nature of the country greatly helps this system. In South Africa it was observed that the ant-hills in a district were generally the same distance apart. You looked at those near you, estimated the distance between them, then counted up the number between you and the object, multiplied the two together, and you got the range.

For example, if you considered the ant-hills fifty yards apart, and there were ten ant-hills between you and the object, ten by fifty yards would equal five hundred yards. Therefore in this case the range would be five hundred yards.

Telegraph poles, posts in a fence, street lamps (especially at night if lighted) and any object laid out at equal intervals, all, are of great assistance in judging distance by measurement.

Second Method.—Now the second method, *i.e.*, " Judging the range by the impression made on the eye by the object."

Sometimes owing to buildings, trees, or the broken nature of the ground, judging across a lake, etc., judging distance by measurement becomes impossible. It is then this second method comes in useful :—

Up to five hundred yards you can generally see a man's face and hands.

Up to eight hundred yards, if moving, a man's arms and legs can be distinguished. If he is further away, his outline alone is visible.

As nowadays troops on active service are clothed in colours, as similar to the ground as possible, the first thing that shows up is a man's face (that is if he is lying quite still watching over cover).

When on the range, say at the five hundred yards firing point, and a man is sent up from the butts, observe what he looks like as he passes the different firing points, one hundred yards, two hundred yards, three hundred yards, four hundred yards. Note how much of him you can distinguish when he leaves the butts, and the various ranges at which his features and uniform become recognisable. Observe also what other objects look like at these ranges.

Third Method.—A combination of both these systems is generally the best. You can check one against the other.

3. Objects Over-estimated.—Objects are liable to be over-estimated :—

 1. If you are kneeling or lying down.

On active service you will always be judging distance in one or other of these positions.

 2. If the ground behind the object is of a similar colour : the object won't show up and will look far away.

 3. Broken ground gives the impression of distance.

 4. Looking across a valley, down a long street, an avenue of trees or a ravine. Anything long and narrow gives the impression of distance.

 5. When the object is in shadow, it is hard to see and it looks further off.

In that case judge on whatever is causing the shadow and allow for the distance between it and the object.

For example, you can just distinguish a man lying in

the shade of a tree, judge on the tree and look at the length of the shadows about yourself and you can estimate how far he is from that tree.

> 6. When the day is hot and heat is rising from the ground.
> 7. When the weather is misty and the light bad.
> 8. When you are unable to see the whole of the object.
> 9. If the wind is strong.

4. Under-estimated.—Objects are liable to be under-estimated :—

> 1. When the ground between you and the object is level, or covered with snow.
> 2. If the sun is behind your back.
> 3. When the object stands out well from the background like a white-washed cottage in a green field.
> 4. Before rain when the atmosphere is clear.
> 5. When looking across water, a narrow valley, a deep gorge or chasm.
> 6. When the object is large.
> 7. Looking upwards or downwards.

Try throwing a stone off the top of a height, and note what a short distance it will descend before striking the ground.

5. Judging Distance by observation of fire.—Another method of finding the range is to watch the strike of the bullets. A considerable volume of fire is generally necessary, but if the distance is not great and the ground dry, less will be required.

Always set your sights *lower* than your estimation of the distance and then raise them by one hundred yards at a time, until the correct range has been ascertained.

6. Estimation of range by movements of enemy.—There is also another method—observing the effect of your shooting on the enemy. If the enemy advance steadily, you are over-estimating the distance. If the enemy advance slowly, and are wavering, you are under-estimating the distance. If the enemy advance by short rushes, you have got the correct distance and the enemy know it.

7. Combined Sights.—At ranges from seven hundred yards to fifteen hundred yards, when an error of one hundred yards in the distance would make the fire non-effective, combined sights are sometimes used. That is half the company would put their sights to fifty yards over the estimated distance and the other half of the company to fifty yards under the estimated distance. This would spread the volume of fire over a greater area of ground and ensure that some portion was effective against the enemy.

8. Fire at an area of ground.—It is frequently necessary to fire at an area of ground, where it is known the enemy are concealed. For this purpose combined sights should certainly be used. An aiming point should be selected and the sighting elevation corrected by observation of fire.

Questions on Lecture

1. Why is it so necessary for a marksman to be also good at judging distance ?

2. Name and describe the three methods of judging distance.

3. When are objects liable to be over-estimated ?

4. When are objects liable to be under-estimated ?

5. Explain how to judge distance by the observation of fire ?

6. Explain how to judge distance by the movements of the enemy.

7. What do you understand by " Combined Sights," and when are they used ?

8. How can you direct fire at an enemy concealed in broken ground ?

INFORMATION

1. Scouts are specially chosen men sent ahead of an army into the enemy's country to gain information and to study the nature of that country.

2. Duties of Scouts.—They send back reports of what they have seen or heard, and on their information the officer commanding the forces bases his plans of operations. If their information is accurately and quickly transmitted, it will facilitate victory ; if inaccurate, or if it arrives too late, perhaps disaster may follow. Now this shows the great responsibility of a scout, how well he must be trained to his work, and with what intelligence and energy he must carry it out. As has been said, a scout is a specially chosen man.

3. Qualities of a Scout.—

(a) A good skirmisher, to approach the enemy unseen.

(b) A good judge of distance, to estimate their position.

(c) A good shot, to protect his own life.

(d) A good signaller, to transmit his information.

(e) He must have a retentive memory, and be able to describe accurately what he has seen or heard.

(f) He must have a good eye for country, and be able to read a map and the stars.

(g) His senses must be acute. Good eyesight and hearing, good sense of touch and smell.

(h) He ought to be daring to the point of rashness, but have a cool head and plenty of common sense.

(i) He must be capable of enduring fatigue.

Scouting is largely a matter of training, training one's powers of observation. Get into the habit of observing things closely. How a horse at the walk leaves a different track to a horse at the trot or the gallop. How the track of an unshod horse differs from one that is shod. Look for peculiarities in a track, try and discover something in it that will enable you to pick it out from a hundred others. For example, the track of a horse that has dropped a shoe will be quite different, to a trained eye, from that of a horse wearing four shoes. The track of a man with nails in his boots is quite different from the track of a man without nails in his boots. A heavily-laden waggon sinks deeper into the ground than one that is lightly laden. The track of a four-wheeled waggon is different from that of a light two-wheeled cart. Here and there it shows double wheelmarks.

Always observe things and you will be surprised at the amount of information you can draw from the most trifling facts. As an old proverb says: "A straw best shows how the wind blows."

4. Most useful kind of information.—Remember the most useful information is that which the enemy does not know you have obtained. If the enemy knows he has been observed, he will alter his plans and your information will be of little use, which has given rise to the saying: "A scout must see without being seen, he must hear without being heard."

Concealment and invisibility therefore are most necessary to a scout. His uniform should not attract attention. Don't clean your belt and buttons. Grease your boots, don't polish them. If you light a fire, be sure it is properly screened and have as little smoke as possible. Don't place it like a bonfire on a hill-side. Be careful in choosing ground for repose, don't lie down near a road or a track, where anyone passing might see you. Get a well concealed spot ; and one must watch while the others rest. Don't all lie down in the same spot, no matter how well concealed. The enemy might surround you, so scatter a bit.

5. If the enemy try to surround you, the best thing to do is to scatter and by different ways get back to a pre-arranged rendezvous or meeting-place. Scouts must always have a rendezvous, so that, in case they are attacked or find it necessary to separate, they can reassemble at a definite point.

6. Calls.—Scouts should always have a signal or group call, so that the leader can bring them together or that they can locate each other in the darkness. But let it not be " The West's awake," or a bit of the latest song. Remember what you want is a call, that won't give away the fact that scouts are about. Now, any ordinary human sound tells one at once that another human being is somewhere near, and if that human sound is a military call, you know there is a soldier about with a rifle in his hand. No, let your signal be to imitate the cry of some animal or the call of some bird.

When arranging the call, just change it sufficiently to enable those in the secret to distinguish it from the real call. Make it either longer or shorter, make a simple variation that can be easily recognised. Let it not be a loud call.

Again, let it be the call of a bird or animal that lives in the district through which you are scouting. Some animals and birds only make a cry when they are disturbed ; a dog will bark if a stranger approaches him. There are other animals that squeal if you suddenly come across them. Now don't imitate those kind of animals, they are liable to put the enemy on the alert, to make him think something is going to happen. No, imitate an animal that likes to make a noise when he is happy and undisturbed. Thus, scouting across marshy or boggy land, imitate, say, the quack of a wild duck or the croak of a frog. Again, scouting through the uplands or meadows, the cry of the corncrake would attract no attention.

7. Imitate a common call, that is the call of an animal or bird that often repeats itself and of which there are plenty in the neighbourhood. A frog will croak all night, and a corncrake cry, so that no matter how often you imitate their sounds it is unlikely to be detected. Anyone expects such an animal or bird to make sounds all night. But if you begin about ten o'clock at night to crow like a cock, or to cackle like a hen that has laid an egg, the enemy will begin to think there are extraordinary fowl about, and will certainly go look for them.

8. Scouts are never sent out aimlessly but for a particular object. It may be to move along the bank of a river from one point to another, to ascertain if the enemy has crossed, to visit a camping ground that the enemy have recently occupied, or to discover if a certain farmhouse is occupied. Whatever it is, scouts must never forget their orders, and that to carry them out must be their first consideration. If you can find out other things, so much the better—a scout should always be observant as he goes along, and all information is useful—but on no account let anything prevent you from carrying out the duty on which you were sent.

9. Remember that negative information is as useful as positive. For example, suppose you were given orders to follow the bank of a river as far as a certain bridge and find out if the enemy has crossed. Now it is just as important to report quickly the negative information,

that no enemy has crossed, as it would be to report, if such were the case, that a whole army had crossed. This is just the sort of information, *viz.*, negative information, that was often looked for during the war in South Africa, when the columns were trying to corner a commando and hedge it in against the blockhouse lines. Morning after morning during one of those big drives, as the circle round the commando grew smaller and smaller, the officer in command anxiously awaited the negative information that no Burghers had slipped through during the night. When it came, he knew all was well, the Burghers were still inside the circle.

10. Country.—In moving through unknown country it is very easy to lose your way. Get the most striking features such as hills, rivers, churches, lakes, railways firmly fixed in your mind. When you reach the brow of a hill, take a good look back and another forward. Impress the main features in your mind before you begin to descend. When you get down into the valley take a look back at the hill you have just left. It rarely happens that a hill will look the same from both sides. In South Africa many a man went astray, because he did not look back after passing through some kopjes. When he tried to return, the country looked so different that he lost his way.

In mountainous countries, like Switzerland, it is a well-known fact that the first thing many men do when they reach the top of a mountain is to give all the surrounding peaks wrong names. They have been toiling up with their eyes on the ground and have not noticed how the appearance of the mountains has been changing at each step, and so they have lost their bearings.

11. Observation Post.—A very useful method of gaining information is to move out at night and occupy a position from which a good view of the enemy's country may be obtained. Stay there all day, and with the help of field glasses observe his movements. But beware of an ambush. Give the enemy credit for having common-sense, and that he knows as well as you do that such and such a position commands a good view of his camp. Avoid walking into a trap, be sure there is another way down besides the way you are going up. Isolated buildings are often traps. Have a good look round before you venture in. It won't do much good to go up into a tower and gain information if you find the door locked when you come down.

There was a case in point during the South African War. Two scouts cantered up to a farmhouse—apparently there was no one about—dismounted and commenced to examine the buildings. They went into an outhouse, but were scarcely inside when they heard the crack, crack, crack of rifles, and bullets came whizzing through the door. They looked about, there was no other exit. The only way out was the way they had come in and the Burghers had the range to a yard, and their rifles trained on to the door. They were caught. What was to be done ? One man made a dash through the door and was knocked over by a volley. The other looked round the outhouse to see if he could find anything to help him. There was a little hay lying about and an old bag in a corner, that was all. But he picked up the bag and filled it with hay and edging up to the door threw it out. The moment the volley rang out, he sprang through the door and made for his horse. The bullets fell all around him, but the range was altered and the Burghers excited, so he reached his horse and got away. But as he thought of his comrade left behind, he bitterly regretted that before dismounting, they had not searched the kopje at the back of the farmhouse.

12. When moving by day avoid being seen by the enemy or the inhabitants. Don't move along roads or in the open.

13. Keep as much as possible to the shade and out of sight. If you do meet with any inhabitants try and gain information, appear friendly, ask them questions, and take them into your confidence by giving misleading information about your own movements.

14. If you perceive the enemy on the march, try and estimate their number by watching how long they take to pass a certain point. It is laid down in the " Field Service Pocket Book " that for each minute the following numbers would approximately go past :—

> Cavalry at the walk in fours 120 each minute.,
> Cavalry at the trot in fours, 250 each minute.
> Artillery guns or waggons at the walk, 5 each minute.
> Infantry in fours, 200 each minute.

Clouds of dust indicate the movement of troops. In some countries fires are lighted to cover these movements, and in countries like South Africa a swarm of locusts looks very like a cloud of dust.

15. In many countries it is customary to light signal fires that send up a flare by night or puffs of smoke by day. To make signals by puffs of smoke light a damp fire and alternately cover and uncover it with a blanket.

The disadvantage of such signals is that it gives away the fact that scouts are moving. The enemy's bivouac fires should be counted either at dusk or early dawn.

16. In scouting before the enemy's outposts, creep up fairly close and there wait until a patrol goes round to visit the groups. Now count how often it is challenged and take the time between each challenge. If you can do this it may be possible to estimate the strength and length of the outpost lines and your information will be of great value.

17. Much information can be gained by visiting vacated camping grounds of the enemy. The state of his commissariat, transport, etc., may be judged by what he has abandoned, *viz.*, animals, carts, food, tents, hospital rubbish, etc. The remains of the fires and the droppings of the animals will indicate the length of time the camp has been empty.

But again beware of a trap. In South Africa a column had often scarcely left its bivouac when a few Burghers would ride in to see what was left behind. On one occasion at least, they received an unpleasant surprise, for the officer commanding a certain column left an ambush behind and when the Burghers rode in they were fired at from seventy yards' range.

18. Reports should be short and to the point. State briefly what you have seen or heard. Only state facts, don't give your opinion. Write clearly; names of towns or persons should be written in capital letters, for example, DUBLIN. Sign the report and put on it your corps, the date, the name of the place where you are writing it, and the actual time it was sent. If you send more than one copy, state to whom and by what means the other copies were sent.

Questions on the Lecture

1. What is a scout?
2. What are the duties of a scout?
3. Name some of the qualities a scout ought to possess.
4. What is the most useful kind of information?
5. How will scouts act if surrounded by the enemy?
6. Why must scouts have a signal or group call?
7. What kind of sound ought this call to be, and why?
8. What is the most important duty of a scout?
9. Is negative information of any value?
10. Why is it necessary to study carefully the main features of the country, as you move along?
11. What is an observation post?
12. What must you avoid when scouting by day?
13. How do you act towards the inhabitants of the country?
14. If you perceive the enemy on the march, how can you estimate his numbers?
15. What is the disadvantage of making signals by lighting fires?
16. What is a good method of scouting in front of the enemy's outpost?

17. Can much information be gained by visiting a vacated camping ground of the enemy ?

18. How should reports be written ?

PROTECTION ON THE MARCH

1. Necessity of Protection.—An army on the march in close formation must be protected from surprise.

2. For this purpose guards are told off, the advance guard to precede the army, the rear guard to follow, and if there is danger of an attack from the right or left there should be flank guards. From whatever point there is the greatest danger of attack, in that direction will be the strongest guard. Therefore, in advancing to the attack, or in pursuit, the advance guard will be the strongest, and in retreat the rear-guard.

The Advance Guard

3. A certain body of men are told off to go ahead and reconnoitre into the enemy's country. This force may be from a *quarter* to an *eighth* of the whole force according to the nature of the country, etc. Cavalry will form part of this force.

4. Duties.—The principal duties of an advance guard are :—

(*a*) To obtain information about the country and the enemy.

(*b*) To protect the main body from surprise.

(c) If the enemy is met in small numbers to drive him in before it and prevent the march from being interrupted.

(d) If the enemy is discovered on the defensive to push in his advance posts and obtain as much information as possible, as to the size of his force and the strength of his position ; but do not get so involved that the main body must come to your rescue.

(e) If the enemy is met advancing with superior forces, to delay his advance till the main body is ready for action.

5. Composition.—An advance guard is divided into two parts :—

    1. The Vanguard.
    2. The Mainguard.

6. The method of sending out an advance guard differs materially with the nature of the country and the troops employed. First a screen of scouts is pushed out, then a connecting file, next the Vanguard, which will consist of about a quarter of the whole advance guard, followed by another connecting file.

7. The duty of the Vanguard is reconnaissance. It will therefore consist when possible of mounted troops. Now comes the main guard, consisting of about half the whole advance guard, and finally a connecting file between the main guard and the main body.

8. The distance between these various sections of the advance guard cannot be laid down. It depends on the

4

nature of the country, whether it is close or open, the danger of surprise, etc. But no portion of the advance guard must ever lose touch with the rest or with the main body. If the country is close, the sections must be nearer together ; if open, the distance will be greater.

The advance guard must be sufficiently far ahead of the main body to allow the latter freedom of action if the enemy should be encountered in force.

9. On the connecting files falls the responsibility of keeping all the sections of the advance guard in touch with each other and with the main body. They are like the links in a chain, if one of them breaks the whole falls to the ground.

10. They must be constantly on the watch for

1. Signals from the front or rear.
2. That the main body does not go astray when a change of direction is made.
3. That the advance guard does not push on too fast and leave the main body behind. It is the main body that regulates the rate of advance, and on the connecting files falls the duty of keeping touch between it and the advance guard. Half of each connecting file must constantly watch towards the enemy and the other half towards the main body.

The Flank Guard

11. If there is danger of the main body being attacked on a flank, that flank must be guarded.

12. The duty of a flank guard is to prevent the enemy getting within striking distance of the flank of the main body.

13. It will march on the flank of the main body. When the latter halts, it halts, but always turns outward to face the point of danger, and occupies the best defensive position at hand. It may also be employed to hold a position until the main body has passed through. For example, to hold the sides of a defile.

The Rear Guard

14. The greatest danger to a defeated force is pursuit. If the commander is relieved from this danger, he can effect a well-ordered retreat, and the vanquished of to-day may be the conqueror of to-morrow.

15. His principal necessity is time—
Time to collect his forces.
Time to put them in order.
Time to remove them to a place of safety.
Time to recover their nerve or " morale."

16. To gain time he detaches a portion of his force to the rear to impede the enemy's advance. As long as this detachment stands as a screen between him and the enemy, he can retreat in safety. But let it once be cut off, surrounded or overwhelmed and the enemy's cavalry will soon be turning that well ordered retreat of the main body into a rout.

Difficulty of Retreat.—Retreat is at all times a difficult matter even when the enemy do not pursue.

Witness, after the battle of Kin-chou, the disorderly retreat of the Russians into Port Arthur. Mr. Nojine describes it as follows in his book : " The Truth About Port Arthur " :—*

" Back, back streamed all. When it was quite dark, when the men of the different units were thoroughly mixed up in the disorderly retreat so that control was impossible, someone shouted that the Japanese Cavalry were coming. What then happened it is difficult to say, but the Infantry opened fire on their own men, there was a lot of miscellaneous shooting and a convoy of wounded from under Tafaskin was taken for the enemy and fired on. Batteries hearing the firing and having no Infantry escort, hurried off to Nangalin. Colonel Laperoff's battery marching ahead in good order was almost swept away by the other batteries galloping on top of it in the dark. All was blind panic until daylight. It was indeed lucky for us the Japanese did not pursue : the results of such pursuit are painful to think of, and the enemy might have got into Port Arthur on the heels of the 4th Division."

17. On the rear guard depends entirely whether or not the main body can reach a place of safety. The Commander finds himself in a very difficult position. He must judge to a nicety how long to hold a position and when it is time to slip away. His principal object will be to take up a position that the enemy cannot avoid in their advance. Then by opening a heavy fire at long range cause them to halt and deploy for the attack, run guns into position, etc. When he sees the enemy have made

---

* London, Mr. John Murray.

all their preparations and are coming on to surround him, he must judge the right moment to close his smaller force and slip away to a new position, if possible leaving the enemy under the impression he is still holding the old. They, on discovering he is gone, will close and resume the pursuit ; but all this takes time, and the main body have been retreating with all speed.

18. The motto of a rear guard commander might well be

" He who fights, then runs away,
Will live to fight another day."

19. To force advancing.—The Rear guard to an advancing force will usually be small, consisting of Infantry and a few mounted men to act as scouts. Their principal duty will be to collect stragglers. If, however, the enemy is strong in cavalry and there is danger of an attack in rear, it will consist of all arms.

Questions on the Lecture

1. Why must an army be protected on the march ?
2. How is it protected ?
3. What is the Advance Guard ?
4. What are its principal duties ?
5. How is the Advance Guard divided ?
6. Describe the general method of sending out an Advance Guard.
7. What is the principal duty of the Van Guard ?
8. What regulates the distance kept between the various portions of the Advance Guard and the Main Body ?

9. Who are responsible that communication is kept up throughout the Advance Guard and with the Main Body ?

10. Name the duties of a Connecting File.

11. When is a Flank Guard necessary ?

12. What are the duties of a Flank Guard ?

13. How does it carry out its duties ?

14. What is the special danger of a defeated force ?

15. What is the greatest necessity ?

16. How is time gained and pursuit averted ?

17. What are the duties of a Rear Guard ?

18. What might be the motto of a Rear Guard ?

19. What are the duties of a Rear Guard to an advancing force ?

PROTECTION WHEN AT REST

Outposts

1. The Necessity for Outposts.—In the previous chapter it has been shown that an army on the march is protected against surprise by guards thrown out all around it. Similarly an army halted for the night or longer must be guarded, that the troops may rest in peace and feel secure.

This is the duty of the Outposts.

2. Duties.—The Outposts consist of a portion of the troops thrown forward all round the camp to watch and ward off a sudden attack by the enemy, to guard all roads and approaches to the camp, to prevent the enemy's scouts obtaining information about the main body, to hold a decided attack of the enemy until the main body have taken up the battle position and are ready to meet it.

3. Composition.—The Outposts may consist of all arms, but at night the brunt of the work must be borne by the Infantry.

4. Distance between Outposts and Main Body.—The distance between the Outpost line and the main body will depend on the strength of the latter and the nature of the country. The Outposts must neither be so far away that the enemy can cut them off, nor so near that in case of attack, the main body would not have time to occupy the battle position before coming under fire.

5. Outpost company moving into position.—When a Company is ordered on Outpost duty, it will move to the ground covered by scouts. It will halt under cover, holding a line *in advance* of the outpost position. The commander, having examined the ground and chosen the positions for the piquets and supports, will issue his orders for the occupation of the position. When the company is posted the screen of scouts will be withdrawn.

6. Division of Company.—An Outpost company is divided into groups, patrols, piquets, supports, and in some cases it may also furnish a detached post.

7. Duties of Commanders of Piquets.—The Commander of the piquet will explain his orders to his piquet.

He will make certain that every man knows

> 1. The direction of the enemy and what cavalry we have in that direction.
> 2. The position of the groups from his own piquet.

3. The position of the piquets on the flanks.
4. The position of the supports.
5. What he is to do in case of attack either by day or by night.
6. The line of retreat.

N.B.—Men are not allowed to take off accoutrements.

The Commander of the piquet will see that the necessary sanitary arrangements are made at once, that the position of the piquet is put in a state of defence and that communications are improved as far as time and circumstance will permit.

In addition, he must see that the groups are properly posted, and explain as follows to each group commander :

1. The amount of frontage, and any special points he is to watch.
2. Where the groups on his right and left are posted.
3. Where his piquet is, and the best way to it.
4. The names of and ranges to prominent objects in view of his post.
5. What he is to do if anyone approaches his post.

8. Groups, method of posting.—A group will consist of three to six men who will find their own sentries and reliefs. Only single sentries need generally be posted within easy distance of the group and if anything occurs the sentry will not feel isolated, but can inform the commander of his group.

A sentry must never lie or sit down except to fire.

9. Explanation of duties by Group Commander.—When posting a sentry, the Commander of the group must carefully explain to him :

What each sentry must know.—

1. The direction of the enemy.
2. The amount of frontage and any special points he is to watch.
3. Where the groups on his right and left are posted.
4. Where his piquet is and the best way to it.
5. The distance to prominent objects.

10. Distance of group from piquet.—A group ought not to be more than about 400 yards from its piquet.

In choosing the best way to the piquet, the commander of the group must be careful that the way chosen will not mask the fire of the piquet or supports.

6. The situation of any detached posts in his neighbourhood.
7. The names of any prominent objects in view of his posts, such as towns, villages, farm-houses, rivers, etc. Where roads and railways lead.

11. Challenging.—A sentry must not challenge loudly, or a watchful enemy may discover the whereabouts of his post. Cover your man with your rifle and then quietly tell him to halt, if he will not halt you can make him do so by pressing your trigger. Observe him first and you have the advantage.

12. Reconnoitring Patrols ; Strength of.—Reconnoitring patrols usually consist of from two to eight men under a N.C.O. They are sent out in front of the outpost position to examine the country, to give timely warning of the enemy's approach or of his preparations to attack, and to communicate with the patrols from the troops on the flanks. The number of patrols will depend on the number of approaches ; there should be one for each, with reliefs. They move out along any roads or tracks for about a mile, and search any likely spots that might conceal the enemy's scouts or where the enemy might mass in preparation for an attack, such as in woods, ravines, etc.

13. Duties of.—Reconnoitring Patrols are sent out for the purpose of observation, not for fighting. Don't let your love of fighting draw you into a small battle on your own account.

14. Duty on getting in touch with the enemy.—If the patrol gets in touch with the enemy or observes something suspicious, the leader will first try and obtain as much definite information as possible and then send back a man to report the same to the commander of his piquet. Don't send back a vague message, write it, if possible, stating the time and place from where it was sent. Let it be short but to the point. Don't state your opinion but only the things you have actually seen or heard. If the message is sent by word, make your messenger repeat it before starting. If written, read it to him, so that if he loses it or finds it necessary to destroy it, he can still tell the substance to the commander of his piquet.

15. When sent out.—Reconnoitring patrols are sent out whenever the commander of the outposts thinks it necessary but especially at dawn and at sunset. They ought if possible to be a mile in advance of the outposts when the dawn breaks. When passing through the groups, the Commander of the patrol must inform the nearest sentry the direction he intends to take.

16. Sentry over Arms.—A sentry is placed over the piquet, to protect it, and to ensure that the orders affecting the piquet issued by its Commander are carried out.

17. Supports ; where placed.—Supports should be placed from a quarter to half a mile in rear of the piquets. They must keep up communication with their piquets and the supports on their right and left. A sentry is posted over each support, and in close country it may be necessary to post communicating sentries between the piquets and supports.

18. Detached Post ; Strength, Duties.—A detached post consists of a group of men (six to twelve, under a chosen leader), separated from the remainder of the piquet line, who have been told off to watch a particular object, for example, to guard an unprotected flank, to prevent the enemy occupying a certain piece of ground either for purposes of observation or for massing troops, to prevent the enemy using a certain ford in a river, etc.

19. Flags of Truce.—On the approach of a flag of truce, the nearest sentries will advance and halt it at such distance that it cannot overlook the Outposts. The Commander of the Outpost company will be informed as to its business. If he gives it permission to pass the Outpost line, the bearer will be blindfolded and led through. No conversation is to take place under any circumstances with the bearer of a flag of truce, except by permission of the officer commanding the Outpost company.

20. Relief.—Outposts are relieved every twenty-four hours, the relief being generally carried out at dawn, so that in case of an attack the outpost line will then be double its ordinary strength.

Dawn is a very favourite hour for attacking a position. To guard against this, the Outposts will stand to arms an hour before sunrise. They will remain under arms until the reconnoitring Patrols have returned and made their reports to the officer commanding the Outposts, who will issue whatever orders he thinks necessary.

To conclude, I shall quote General Sir Ian Hamilton's remarks on the Japanese Outposts at Fen-huang-chung during the pause after their victory on the Yalu River :—*

" I thought the selection of the ground for the Outposts was admirable. Facilities for observation, resistance, counter-attack or retirement were combined with economy of men. The trenches were generally along the crest line of low hills, the Infantry in front, the guns a few hundred yards behind on a higher level. There were splinter-proof shelters everywhere, with tunnelled-passages leading out from them to the trenches or gun pits. . . . In all the Infantry trenches, there were niches cut at intervals of a yard for ammunition. Ravines were filled up, where they could afford cover to the enemy, and woods were cut down and turned into abattis."

N.B.—To make abatti obstacles, trees are cut down and the branches lopped and sharpened.

---

* "A Staff-Officer's Scrap Book." By General Sir Ian Hamilton. By permission of the publisher, Mr. Edward Arnold.

Questions on Lecture

1. Why are Outposts necessary ?

2. What are the duties of Outposts ?

3. What is the composition of Outposts ?

4. What regulates the distance between the Outpost lines and the Main body ?

5. How does a company ordered on Outpost duty move into position ?

6. How is a company divided for Outpost duty ?

7. What are the duties of the commander of a piquet ?

8. What are the methods of posting groups ?

9. What must the commander of a group explain to the sentry ?

10. How far ought a group to be from its piquet ?

11. How should a sentry challenge ?

12. What is the strength of a Reconnoitring Patrol ?

13. What are the duties of a Reconnoitring Patrol ?

14. If a Reconnoitring Patrol gets in touch with the enemy, how will it act ?

15. When are Reconnoitring Patrols sent out ?

16. Who keeps watch over the piquet ? What are his duties ?

17. Where are the Supports placed ?

18. What is a detached post ? What is its strength, what its duties ?

19. What are the duties of Sentries on the approach of a Flag of Truce ?

20. Why are the Outposts relieved at dawn ?

THE BATTLE (Part I)

The Attack (*General remarks*)

1. To advance is to win; to advance is to win! That is the secret of war, of every war since the world began, as it must be of every war till the world is ended.

To advance is to win; to advance is to win! All your training in shooting, in marching, skirmishing, cover and eyesight has but one object: to teach you to advance and win.

2. To win, you must close with your enemy. To win, you must charge home with the bayonet.

The bayonet says the last word—Victory! but when the bayonet gleams you are very near the enemy.

3. Now, how did you get there, so near and yet unhurt?

Looking back you might wonder, until slowly it would come to you how every time you advanced some one had opened fire to help you. Sometimes it was men near you in the firing line; sometimes it was the supports; again it was a machine gun posted just in the rear (you remember the bullets screaming overhead and how it made you nervous at first). Whenever you moved, there always seemed to be a friend at hand, a kind of guardian angel, ready and willing to support you, to open fire and upset the enemy's aim.

This gave you confidence and as you advanced, your confidence grew and grew; until you began to feel you were a bigger man than the enemy, which of course is the best way to feel before attacking any man.

Now do you realise the meaning of rifle fire ? Now do you understand its use ?

4. Why do men fire ?

Men fire to help others to advance.

Men are ordered to fire, not so much with the object of killing the enemy, as with the object of preventing the enemy from delaying the advance of our own firing line.

That is the thing to remember.

Make the enemy keep his head down and our firing line can advance, and finish him with the bayonet.

That is called giving covering fire.

5. But covering fire to be effective and helpful must be well directed and this shows the necessity for your training and practice in shooting.

This is why you are taught fire discipline and control, so that the fire may be directed where it is most needed.

Unless a company has a good shooting average, its fire will be of little value.

We ought all learn to be marksmen.

6. A marksman on service is the man who makes the first hit at an unknown range.

7. Now let us imagine we are watching the advance of the firing line, from the time it extends until it reaches the enemy's trenches. In skirmishing order under cover of the fire of the machine guns and supports it advances steadily from fire position to fire position, until a line is occupied close to the enemy from which further advance will generally be impossible until the fire of the enemy has been weakened.

This is the critical moment in the attack.

Success or failure is in the balance.

The firing line opens a rapid fire, more and more re-inforcements come up, an intense fire is heaped on the trenches until gradually the fire of the enemy weakens and fails.

Bayonets are fixed, the order for the assault is given, and with a mighty shout, the men spring up, and sweeping forward, carry the position.

8. They then get quickly on the defensive and prepare to hold what they have won against all attempts by the enemy to recapture it.

Questions on the Lecture

1. What is the secret of success in War ?
2. How is the victory won ?
3. What protects your life in the advance ?
4. What is the principal use of fire ?
5. Why is it so necessary to control fire ?
6. Define a marksman for service purpose.
7. Describe the advance of the firing line ?
8. What do the firing line do when the position is captured ?

THE BATTLE—(Part II)

The Company in the Attack

In an attack the company will not be acting alone, but in co-operation with the other companies of the battalion and the remainder of the troops employed.

When the company has assembled, the Commander will tell you what is known about the position and strength of the enemy and what part the company will take in the attack. He will also explain what the remainder of the battalion have been detailed to do.

Let us suppose that our company has been detailed as part of the firing line.

1. The advance of the battalion will be covered by scouts, and when the Colonel considers that they are sufficiently far ahead, he will order the companies detailed as the firing line to 'commence the attack.

2. To guard against shell fire I shall move you off in a shallow formation either in column of route, file or in company column. The exact formation will depend on the nature of the country.

3. The Company will advance as long as possible in a shallow formation and with luck we ought to get to within about 1,400 yards of the enemy without having to extend.

When to advance in close formation is no longer safe I shall halt you under cover and extend you.

4. But first I shall point out the part of the enemy's position we are to attack, the amount of frontage allotted to the company and how the attack will be carried out.

5

5. Having finished my explanation I shall detail 1 and 2 sections as firing line and 3 and 4 sections as supports.

No. 1 section will then extend and commence the advance. The remaining three sections will also extend, but will remain behind cover.

When No. 1 section has advanced about 200 yards I shall order No. 2 section to advance, and when No. 2 section has advanced 200 yards I shall order No. 3 section to advance, and No. 4 will follow No. 3 at the same distance.

6. Now why have I left an interval of 200 yards between each section ?   Because 200 yards is the length of ground searched by the forward throw of shrapnel and I want to ensure that shrapnel aimed at one section will not also hit another section.   Section commanders must see this distance is kept, but of course if by reducing this distance or extending it, a little better cover can be obtained, the section commander should make use of it.

7. Again, I shall tell each section commander that he is to advance his section simultaneously with that in front.

As soon as the leading section jumps up to advance, the commanders of the other three sections will order their sections to do likewise. When the leading section halts and lies down, the remaining sections will halt and lie down.

8. Now why should the four sections advance together ? Because each advance will give the enemy but one chance of firing at all four sections, whereas if each section advanced separately the enemy could concentrate all their fire on each section in turn,

The commander will generally be with the supports until they are absorbed into the firing line.

Now the advance will be made from fire position to fire position, each successive position being chosen beforehand by the officer in charge of the firing line.

9. As each section advances, it will occupy the fire position vacated by the section in front. It will strengthen that position and make of it a line of defence so that if the firing line has to retire it can fall back on a series of entrenched positions. The Japanese used this method of advance with great success.

10. Fire will be opened when it is no longer possible to advance without heavy loss.

11. The Company Commander will judge when fire is to be opened and no one is to commence firing until he gives the order.

12. Now the firing line will continue to advance, being reinforced when necessary by the remainder of the firing line, and later by the supports, until gradually a strong firing line is built up within rushing distance of the enemy (200 yards). Then when the fire of the enemy begins to weaken and fail, bayonets are fixed, the order for the assault is given, and with a mighty shout everyone jumps up and charges the position.

13. The moment the position is captured don't lose your heads, put yourselves under any officer or leader who is at hand, get on the defensive and prepare to resist the attempt that the enemy is sure to make to retake it.

There are a few other points to be observed in the attack.

14. The chief danger beyond 1,400 yards is artillery fire. Against artillery fire we adopted a shallow formation such as company columns, columns of route or file.

When the danger gets pronounced you will be extended.

But how are we to cross unaimed zones of fire ?

15. What is an unaimed zone of fire ?

Have you ever seen rain falling from a cloudless sky. No, it sounds like magic, but something like that will happen, when you are crossing a zone of unaimed fire, only it will not be rain or hailstones, it will be bullets.

A shower of bullets coming from space !

Well, not exactly, they must come from somewhere, as a matter of fact they are caused by the enemy firing (at long range) against troops they can see and hitting you whom they can't see.

You might describe it as very bad shooting, but the bullets are real ; something has got to be done.

16. Double, double, double, that's the way to cross the trouble. We must double forward until the bullets are left behind.

17. The fire unit is the section.

Fire will be opened by sections and controlled as long as possible by the section commander.

18. Fire will usually be deliberate and at the target giving the most trouble.

19. Fire control.—Fire will be withheld as long as possible.

" The rate of fire should not excel a man's best rate, *i.c.* the greatest number of rounds that he can fire with reasonable accuracy.

The rate of fire will depend, therefore, on the size of the target, the man's eyesight and training in quick and accurate aim."*

20. Men must learn to obey accurately all fire orders received, and in the absence of fire orders to carry on the fight with coolness and judgment.

21. Rapid Fire.—Keep rapid fire for a good opportunity, such as a fleeing enemy, cavalry, a large target, and before the assault to help the supports to advance.

22. Rapid fire is difficult to control, so the number of rounds to be fired will be mentioned by the section commander when giving the order, for example : " At the men crossing the road, 400 yards, 3 rounds rapid."

You would set your sights to 400 yards, fire your 3 rounds, cease fire, load again and wait for a fresh order.

The advance should be rapid and strong with plenty of ammunition left when you get to close quarters.

We are certain to meet with obstacles and must overcome them as best we can. The Bulgarian method of crossing the barbed wire round Adrianople is well worth remembering. They say there was enough barbed wire round Adrianople to encircle the earth. In the final assault the Bulgarians were held up by barbed wire entanglements until one man threw his great coat on the

---

* *Vide* " Summary, Infantry in Battle."

wire, more followed his example and in a few minutes the men ran over the entanglements on a carpet of coats.

23. The orders before assault are, " Cease Fire ! Fix bayonets ! "*

Assault.—Before the assault, bayonets are fixed, and when you fix your bayonet, charge your magazine. Before you charge your enemy, charge your magazine.

24. When the order for the assault is given, spring up together and rush the enemy. The assault is like a tug-of-war, it's a case of all together boys or the attack will fail.

To succeed you must charge as if you intended to go a mile beyond the trenches.

25. Covering fire and mutual support.—Last of all we must not forget that it is the duty of every man taking part in the attack to help the advance of his comrades by every means in his power. Mutual support is the secret of a successful attack.

How do you give this mutual support ? *By covering fire.* If the attack is over undulating ground, the firing line will rely for covering fire on the supports and reserves, who will fire over their heads.

But if the attack is over level ground, the supports and reserves will not be able to fire, so that each section of the firing line must support the remainder. This can best be done by the fire of one company covering the advance of another.

---

* *Vide* " Infantry Training."

Questions on the Lecture

1. Who precedes the battalion into action ?

2. In what formation does the company advance to the attack ?

3. When is the Company ordered to extend ?

4. What does the officer commanding each company explain before extending his company ?

5. How is the company sub-divided for the advance ?

6. Why should there be an interval of 200 yards between sections ?

7. How should the four sections advance ?

8. Why should the sections advance together ?

9. Why should the succeeding sections strengthen each fire position ?

10. When do you commence firing ?

11. Who gives the first order to open fire ?

12. Describe the final stages of the attack.

13. What do you do when the position is captured ?

14. How do we guard against artillery fire ?

15. What causes an unaimed zone of fire ?

16. How do you cross such zones of fire ?

17. What is the fire unit and who controls it ?

18. What is the usual rate of fire ?

19. What do you understand by a man's " Best rate " of fire ?

20. In the absence of fire orders, what should men do ?

21. When is rapid fire used ?

22. How is rapid fire controlled ?

23. What does each man do before the assault ?

24. How is the assault carried out ?

25. What is the duty of every man on the field of battle ?

THE BATTLE—(Part III)

Local and General Reserves

If the company is not employed as a firing line and supports, it will be detailed as a local reserve or part of the general reserve.

1. Local Reserves.—The local reserves follow in rear of the supports, a certain proportion is allotted to each section of the firing line. Their duty is to cover with rifle fire the advance of the firing line, and to support it against local counter attacks.

2. A local counter attack is a sudden attack by the enemy on a part of the firing line.

For example, a part of the firing line has captured a hill from which it can pour a heavy fire on the enemy's trenches. It is plain that if it is allowed to establish itself there, the enemy must retire from that portion of the position. But the enemy has no wish to retire, instead he makes a determined counter attack on the hill.

This is the opportunity of the Local Reserves, they come to the assistance of their comrades on the hill, and together they force back the enemy.

It is the duty of the local Reserve to assist the Firing Line by every means in their power.

3. General Reserve.—The General Reserve will be at the disposal of the Commander-in-Chief.

It will consist of about half the whole force and be composed of all arms.

4. To defeat a powerful enemy, our object must be to deceive him as to the real point of attack by keeping him vigorously employed elsewhere; then when the right moment has come, to throw in superior forces at the point where it is intended to force home the attack, and, before the enemy has recovered, rush the position.

This is the duty of the General Reserve, but it will also be used to pursue a defeated enemy, nip a counter-attack in the bud, or for any other purpose the General Officer commanding may think necessary.

5. Counter-Attack.—A counter-attack is a sudden attack by the defence, when they judge the attack is wavering and spent, or when they believe the attacking troops have placed themselves at a disadvantage.

For example, if you were beating a dog with a stick, and the stick broke, and the dog suddenly bit you in the leg, that would be a most successful counter-attack on the part of that dog.

Assault of Hill 125, R.-J. War.—The following is an account from "The Truth About Port Arthur," by M. Nojine, of the assault by the Japanese on one of the defences of Port Arthur on the 27th July, 1904.

"At seven o'clock fifteen companies could be seen advancing in columns in the valley. . . . They were moving towards Hill 125, and as soon as they came under fire, they could be seen to extend in successive lines, one battalion remaining in reserve. Having extended, they steadily and quickly advanced to the attack in eleven lines. The distance between their firing line and Hill 125 quickly decreased. . . ."

At length the Russians opened fire by volleys.

" Volley followed volley, and the machine guns vomited bullets. The enemy's firing line could be seen to falter, then the second line melted into it. On they came. Our volleys rang out more frequently, but did not stop the advance; the third line melted into the remnant of the first two. . . . The Japanese were close on us. As a line began to waver, it was reinforced and carried forward by the next in rear, and so it went on, fresh lines after lines appearing as if there was no end to them.

The Crescent of the Attack.—" Their firing line began to crawl up the hill *from all sides*. Volleys gave way to ' Independent ' crack, crack, crack all round and the deafening rat-tat-tat of the machine guns. Now the range was point blank, the crew of our machine guns were all down—but—the enemy were repulsed.

" While they gathered down below for a fresh effort, their guns fired a hail of high explosive shells on to our trenches and did their work so well that our trenches were thick with wounded. Their Infantry rallied and again came on in swarms. . . . Burnevitch sent for reinforcements, and the men expecting they would come at every moment held out for another hour. At last an order was received ' to retire.' . . . The withdrawal was effected." Hill 125 was in the hands of the Japanese, the fate of Port Arthur was sealed.

Questions on the Lecture

1. What is the duty of a Local Reserve ?
2. What is a local counter-attack by the enemy ?

3. What is the size of the general reserve ?
4. What is the object of having a general reserve ?
5. What is a counter attack ?

THE BATTLE—Part IV

Night Attack

1. When the approaches to a position are very open and are well covered by the guns of the defence, it will probably be impossible to attack by daylight. The attacking force would be subject to a heavy fire from the opening of the attack and would never be able to reach close range in sufficient numbers to master the fire of the enemy and to carry the position. In such cases the position must be carried by night.

In brief, the objective of a night attack is to carry a position too strong to be captured by day and to entrench yourself there, under cover of darkness.

2. Fighting by night is much more difficult than fighting by day.

There is the danger of losing one's way to the exact point where one hopes to drive home the assault. The danger of arriving there too early or too late. The danger of losing touch with the troops on your right and left. The danger of mistaking friend for foe.

The difficulties are great, but both during the South African War and the late Balkan Wars, night marches and night attacks were carried out with marked success.

3. The secret lay in the organization. The orders were brief and clear. Each man was told what was expected of him and no more. The ground was carefully reconnoitred, not only by scouts and the officers who were to guide the columns to the attack, but by whole companies, so that as many men as possible knew the ground beforehand.

4. Method of carrying out a night attack.—The general method of carrying out a night attack is as follows :—

> (a) The Commander of the forces appoints a place of assembly and orders the troops detailed to take part in the attack to meet there at a certain hour.

> (b) When they have assembled he issues his detailed instructions, and each company officer explains them to his men. He tells them the object and direction of the attack ; the point where the company will deploy ; the formation in which they will attack ; what is expected of the company ; what the company will do in case the enemy is not surprised.

To be able to approach the enemy unobserved is the great advantage of attacking by night.

Therefore rifles will not be loaded but the magazines will be charged and cut-offs closed. No one is to fire without an express command. The bayonet alone must do the work. In absolute silence the company advances to the attack, no striking of matches, no lighting of pipes. If obstacles are met with that cannot be passed, the company will lie down until a gap has been cleared.

To conclude I will quote from " A Staff-Officer's Scrap Book "* an account of the night attack on the night of the 1st and 2nd September, 1904, when the first Japanese army under General Kuroki were endeavouring to cut the Russian lines of communications. There was a little hill called Manjuyama, which was a great obstacle to the Japanese advance. Manjuyama is about 75 feet high, 300 yards long and 20 yards broad on the top. It's distinctive feature was that it was a landmark in the sea of kaoliung crops (ten feet to twelve feet high) which surrounded it and caused all eyes to be turned towards it. Manjuyama was exposed to the Russian guns from three directions. It was impossible therefore to carry the hill in daylight.

" As soon, however, as the crepuscule had deepened into profound obscurity, which last night preceded the rising of the moon he (Okasaki) advanced his brigade through the kaoliung to within rushing distance.

" Each battalion† moved with one company in line, leading, followed at close intervals by the other three companies at deploying intervals. The direction was kept by the compasses of the officers. The signal for the onslaught was to be the rising of the moon.

" It was nearly ten p.m. when the first pale moonbeams stole across the battle field and no sooner did Manjuyama's ridge emerge ghost-like at that summons from the darkness than the 30th Regiment under that brave old Colonel Baba charged into its northern face with a tremendous

---

* General Sir Ian Hamilton. By permission of the publisher, Mr. Edward Arnold.

† A Japanese Battalion consists of four companies.

Banzai yell. They made good their footing and then came the turn of the 16th Regiment, which also dashed in fiercely and effected a lodgment on the hillock's southern slopes. But the Russians here were stout fellows, although not very numerous or strongly entrenched, and those holding the centre part of the position were not at all inclined to say Amen to the Japanese Banzai. Till midnight, confusion and passionate fighting took place backwards and forwards over the shell-scarred features of this little rice-cake hill, about which hour the last handful of Russians holding on round a small tumulus on the summit were fairly forced back into the surrounding sea of kaoliung. Hardly had the Japanese realized that they were masters of the position when two of the enemy's battalions made a determined counter-attack against the right flank of the 30th Regiment. Had these two battalions come as a reinforcement a few minutes earlier, whilst their own men were still maintaining their grip on the summit, the results of the night's fighting might have been different. As it was, the counter-attack was repulsed after half-an-hour's fighting."

Questions on the Lecture

1. When is it necessary to make a night attack ?
2. What are the disadvantages ?
3. How can these difficulties be overcome ?
4. Describe the general method of carrying out a night attack ?

THE BATTLE—Part V

The active defence

1. To advance is to win : that is true, but there are times when it is not possible to commence operations by a forward movement. An army must mobilize, and the side that is the quicker to mobilize will be the first in the field.

In the recent war between Turkey and the Balkan League, Bulgaria commenced mobilizing before Turkey.

The Turks set to and mobilized as fast as possible, but the Bulgarians finished first and, assuming the offensive, forced the Turks to act on the defensive.

It was a different reason that directed the Russians to act on the defensive in their war with Japan.

They had an advantage in ground.

They knew that to invade Manchuria the Japanese must advance through Korea and they had in their possession that hilly ground which rising abruptly from the banks of the Yalu River forms a natural barrier between Manchuria and Korea.

Korea is a long narrow strip of country running out into the sea like a branch from a tree. At the point where it joins Manchuria, there is a chain of mountains with the Yalu River about a mile wide flowing at their base. It was on these mountains the Russians prepared positions and awaited attack. The Yalu River though broad is shallow and full of islands and sandbanks.

But although the position was naturally strong and well

held, the Japanese turned their left flank and forced the Russians to retreat.

Why were the Japanese successful ?

Because the defence was passive, not active.

When I say the defence was passive I mean the Russians sat in their trenches and made no attempts to disturb the Japanese, to upset their arrangements and to discover their plans for attack.

It is reported that during the four or five days the Japanese were massing in preparation for the attack, the Russians never sent a single cavalry patrol across the river to discover their movements.

Such defensive action will ever be futile.

2. The defence of a position should be active, full of surprises, full of pit-falls that wear out the enemy and dishearten him. His movements should be forestalled ; every inch of the ground disputed. This will cause him to use up his reserves earlier than he intended. It will leave him without sufficient reserves at the critical moment of the attack, *i.e.*, when he is endeavouring to carry the position by assault.

Now let us consider the different duties of the defence, and more particularly the part the company will play.

3. An army in defence is divided into firing line and supports, local reserves and general reserves. The number of men in each portion of the firing line will depend on the nature of the ground, some parts of a position are easier to defend than others.

The supports will equal about a half to a fifth of the firing line.

The Local Reserve will be as strong as the firing line and supports put together.

The General Reserve will not be less than half the whole force. Now let us suppose that our battalion has been told off as part of the firing line and supports, and that our company has been allotted a certain portion of the ground to defend.

4. How shall we defend it? By making trenches and providing communicating trenches with the supports in rear. By cleaning the foreground of everything that prevents a clear field of fire, demolishing buildings, filling in ditches, etc. Next, obstacles will be erected in unlooked for places, and barbed wire entanglements will be constructed.

5. In fact, everything will be done to make the approach to the position as difficult as possible, but gaps through which the local counter attacks can be launched, should be left in the barbed wire and in the lines of obstacles: these gaps should be defended by small trenches placed just in rear.

The Turks in Adrianople neglected this precaution.

The wire entanglements were unbroken, making it impossible for the Turks to get out; and when the Bulgarians began to mass before the final assault, in some dead ground only 500 yards from the main trenches, the Turks could not get at them.

Ranges should be taken to all prominent objects, and the distances posted up in the trenches.

6. When the position is prepared, the firing line will

6

retire into the trenches in rear, and rest until required.
Before a battle everyone ought to take as much sleep as
possible and only a thin line of skirmishers or sentries
will be on the watch in the main trenches.

7. The cavalry will be out in front and will be the first
to come in contact with the enemy. They will endeavour
to mislead him as to the extent and nature of the main
position, and then gradually retire to the flanks.

8. The machine guns will take up positions commanding
all roads and positions where the enemy might place his
guns. When the attack develops we shall be ordered to
man the trenches.

9. The right movement for opening fire cannot be laid
down. It will depend on the strength of the defences,
the strength and fighting qualities of the enemy and how
far we can make use of the element of surprise.

Premature opening of fire discloses the position and has
little effect on the enemy. Fire should not be opened
until the enemy present a good mark.

10. The principal use of fire in defence is to prevent
the advance of the attacking troops.

Watch for opportunities for enfilade fire. They are sure
to occur, the enemy attacking one portion of the position
will often expose himself to enfilade fire from another.
That would be an opportunity for rapid fire.

If we are pressed, the supports will help us; and remember that behind the supports there is a local reserve,
specially told off to assist each portion of the defence.

11. What is the duty of the Local Reserve ? It is to make the enemy pay for his mistakes and to assist the firing line.

The enemy can make mistakes in many ways; for example by exposing his flank to enfilade fire or by leaving too big a gap between his firing line and supports. This would give the local reserve a chance of charging down on the firing line and driving it back in confusion before it could be reinforced.

12. The general reserve will make the decisive counter-attack when the enemy has been repulsed. It will generally consist of all arms and will not be less than one half the whole force. The general reserve is the striking force of the defence. It will be held in readiness until the opportunity arises of dealing the enemy a crushing blow.

13. The Decisive counter-attack ; most favourable moment for.—This will generally occur when the enemy have thrown all their reserves into the firing line and in attempting to carry the trenches have been repulsed. At this moment they don't quite know what to do. They are disheartened and can't decide whether it is better to advance or retire. If the counter-attack suddenly bursts upon them and threatens to cut off their retreat, it will help them materially to make up their minds. They will go, and the more vigorously the counter-attack presses forward, the faster they will go. But the object of the counter-attack is not only to make the enemy retire and retire quickly, it is, if possible, to make them break and retire in confusion. Then with the Infantry, supported by the machine guns, on their heels and the Cavalry harassing their flanks and endeavouring to head them off —well—I would rather not be the enemy.

The following is a description from Mr. Maxwell's book : " From the Yalu to Port Arthur,"* of the defences of a hill in front of the village of Shyaoyansui during the battle of Lia-yang, 31st August, 1904 :—

" The low hill with the three broad crests and a gentle slope from the South. Three or four hundred yards from the foot of this slope ran a triple line of trous de loup or circular pits, ten feet deep with a sharp stake in the middle of each pit. Nearly a mile long, the line of defensive works was broken at intervals to afford passage to the Russians. In these gaps were wire entanglements and chevaux de frise, and behind these were trenches held by riflemen, while in front were mines. At the foot of the hill were other wire entanglements and on top of the incline commanding every yard of approach ran a deep trench with a shallow trench immediately behind. Along the summit were two lines of trenches traversed at right angles, and on the ridge beyond were emplacements for guns."

Questions on the Lecture

1. When does an army act on the defensive ?
2. How should a position be defended ?
3. Describe how an army is divided in defence.
4. Describe how a company will prepare its portion of the position.

---

* Published by Hutchinson & Co., London.

5. Why should gaps be left in the barbed wire and lines of obstacles ?

6. What will the company do when their portion is prepared ?

7. How do the cavalry act in defence ?

8. Where will the machine guns be placed ?

9. What governs the opening of fire ?

10. What is the principal use of fire in the defence ?

11. What is the duty of the Local Reserve in defence ?

12. What troops make the decisive counter-attack ?

13. When is the best moment to launch the decisive counter-attack ?

PRESERVATION OF HEALTH

Introduction.—Formerly very little was known about diseases and few precautions were taken against them. When a man got ill, if he was a strong man he recovered, if not he died. No one could help him, because no one knew quite what was wrong. Nowadays all diseases of a preventative and contagious kind are found to be caused by microbes, that is, insects so small that they cannot be seen except through a microscope. These microbes float about in the air, rest on food, fall into water. They are like the seeds of the thistle, blown about by the wind and take root and grow wherever they alight ; and as a farmer will cut his thistles before they are ripe and the seed has time to scatter, so by taking certain sanitary precautions, principally cleanliness, microbes can be prevented from scattering and increasing in the human body and in human food. Act on the old saying that prevention is better than cure. In cities and towns, the corporations and Town Councils look after the health of the people. They see that the water supply is good, that the streets are cleaned and refuse removed, etc. The health of the people is cared for, they have little to do for themselves. But on active service things are very different. Here, if we don't look after ourselves, there is no one else to do so.

Little attention was paid to these matters in former days, and the armies suffered accordingly, as the following examples mentioned in "The Manual of Sanitation" bear witness :—

" During the Peninsular War three times as many were lost by sickness as by wounds, and more than twice the strength of the whole army passed through the hospitals on account of disease. . . . the United States army was decimated by sickness before it ever sailed for the area of operations during the recent war with Spain. In the recent campaign in South Africa 69 men per 1,000 died of disease and 746 per 1,000 of strength were at one time or other non-effective from sickness. In the year 1802 a French expedition to San Domingo lost 50,000 men out of 58,000 men, from it (Yellow Fever), in the course of four months."

Men who were present during the Russo-Japanese War estimate that the Japanese lost 60,000 men by disease. The diseases most likely to attack an army are, Enteric Fever, Dysentery, Diarrhœa, Cholera, Malaria, Yellow Fever, Plague, Malta or Mediterranean Fever, Typhus Fever, Scurvy, Consumption.

Certain diseases occur more often in one country than in another. India is the home of cholera, South Africa of enteric fever, West Coast of Africa of malaria fever, the West Indies and South America of yellow fever. Scurvy is liable to attack troops in a besieged place where fresh food supplies cannot be obtained. Typhus fever may occur in any place where dirt abounds. Consumption, while very much on the decrease in England since the passing of several health acts, is still on the increase in Ireland. There is no necessity in this lecture to describe these diseases in detail. It will be sufficient to point out that the same preventative or sanitary measures apply to all.

1. Foul air, impure water, uncleanliness of any kind is a sure breeding place for disease. Wherever these conditions are found, there will microbes breed, and the diseases most common to the locality break out.

Dirt therefore is the commencement of all diseases, and to fight against dirt wherever met is the duty of every soldier.

Water.—The drinking of impure water is a very easy way of contracting disease.

2. Generally speaking, the deeper the source of supply, the better will the water be. Therefore, water from a deep well is much safer than from one that is shallow. Again, always try and get the purest supply available.

3. Water in the centre of a river or lake is much purer than near the banks. River water is very uncertain;

it is so liable to be contaminated while passing through the towns situated on its banks.

4. Mountain streams give good water, and rain water caught in *clean* vessels is quite safe.

5. The responsibility of deciding if water is fit for use, only falls on the individual volunteer when on detachment duty. Then he must decide for himself.

6. The best way out of the difficulty is to get as pure water as possible and boil it. Keep it at the boil for five minutes. First, rinse out your water-bottle with the boiling water to make sure it is clean. There is no use boiling the water if the bottle is dirty. Next, fill the bottle straight from the tin in which it was boiled. If you do this you need not be afraid to drink it.

7. Water that tastes sweet is often bad. This kind of water is frequently found in a well, in a farmyard, because impure matter has soaked into it. Good water is generally insipid and tasteless. Men must learn to control their thirst. If not, they must only take the consequences. Don't rush and drink the first water you see. I remember one day in South Africa, stopping at a dam to water the horses ; the order was given not to drink the water, but before they could be stopped, two men had dipped their water-bottles and were drinking. They were ordered to stop before they had taken more than a mouthful, but both got enteric fever and one died in a little over a week.

8. A warm drink is much better for quenching thirst

than a cold drink.   It is not so pleasant to swallow but it is much safer.

9. Never eat snow, it gives fever at once and also an unquenchable thirst.   You may boil snow, but if possible find a spring and use it instead.

10. Food should be kept covered from dust and insects, in a clean cool place, where there are no smells, and plenty of fresh air.   A clean box covered with gauze and hung in the shade would do very well.

11. Food in a state of decomposition is very dangerous. If on opening a tin it is found to smell badly, bury it.   It is a case of burying the tin or being buried yourself.   No amount of cooking will make it safe.   You may kill the microbes that caused the trouble, but such a tin is poisoned and it is the poison that will kill you.

12. Tinned food must be examined carefully before being used and any tins badly dented, rusty, etc., should be rejected.

13. Air.—Fresh air is an essential to health.   Rooms in which there is no ventilation become loaded with gases and vapours given off from the lungs and bodies of the occupants.

14. The best way to ventilate a room is to leave the top of the windows open, as bad air always rises to the top and will thus pass out.

Overcrowded, badly ventilated rooms are sure places for spreading diseases like consumption.

15. If on coming in from the fresh air, a room feels stuffy, it is a sign that it is not properly ventilated, and you must look for the cause and remedy it.

16. Personal cleanliness, clothing.—At all times, even on active service, one ought to cultivate habits of personal cleanliness. It helps very much to keep one in health. One feels as well again after a good bath.

17. The feet must receive particular attention, as dirt leads to sore feet, the worst enemy of a soldier.

18. Clean hands and finger nails are important, as they touch the food you eat.

19. Clothing should be kept clean. It is not much use taking a bath if you put on a dirty shirt. Keep your clothing sweet and clean, particularly your under garments, keep them in repair, especially socks. Holes in socks give sore feet, and socks badly darned are almost worse.

20. If vermin get into clothes on active service, they are easiest destroyed by boiling the articles infected.

21. The use of a comrade's mess tin, drinking from his water bottle, etc., are very common methods of spreading disease.

22. Spitting and the use of other men's pipes is a very common way of spreading consumption. In the one case the spittle dries and the microbes float about in the air, in the other the microbes are sucked in straight from the pipe. Spitting is at all times a dirty and objectionable habit.

Questions on the Lecture

1. In general what is the cause of all disease ?
2. Is water from a well generally good ?
3. What part of a lake or stream holds the best water ?
4. Is rain water fit for use ?
5. How can you make water safe for drinking ?
6. Describe how you would do so ?
7. Does good water taste different to bad ?
8. Why does a hot drink quench one's thirst better than a cold drink ?
9. Will eating snow do you any harm ?
10. How should food be kept ?
11. Will boiling make a tin of decomposed food safe ?
12. What must you do before opening tinned food ?
13. Why is fresh air so necessary ?
14. How would you ventilate a room ?
15. How would you test the freshness of a room ?
16. Why must personal cleanliness be encouraged ?
17. Why should particular attention be paid to the feet ?
18. Why is it so important to keep the hands and finger nails clean ?
19. How should clothing be kept ?
20. How can you kill vermin in clothing ?
21. Is it any harm to drink from another man's mess-tin or water-bottle, or to use his pipe ?
22. Why is spitting so objectionable ?

SIMPLE REMEDIES IN CASE OF ACCIDENTS

General Remarks.—Accidents are so liable to occur, both in camp and on active service, that some short remarks on their general treatment will not be out of place.

Slight injuries may become serious if neglected or wrongly treated, and more serious accidents may end fatally from the same causes.

The following suggestions have been compiled from the " Field Service Pocket Book " and other sources.

They put briefly what to do in case of accidents, but remember they are only intended for emergencies. *In all cases medical aid should be summoned as quickly as possible.*

1. Loss of Consciousness.

(a) If a man faints, lay him on his back with the head lower than his body, loosen the clothes about the neck. Sprinkle the head and neck with cold water. Give a little stimulant.

2. (b) If a man falls on his head, for example, out of a cart, and becomes unconscious, or if his stomach gets ill after such a fall, he must be treated differently. Give no stimulants. Let him rest his head low and apply warmth to his body.

3.　　(c) In the case of sunstroke, carry the patient to the coolest place available, and give him plenty of fresh air. Keep the head raised, take the clothes off the upper part of the body and bathe his head, neck and chest with cold water. In bad cases it may be necessary to bathe the whole body. Give no stimulant.

4. Bandage in case of emergency.—In case of emergency a bandage may be made from any clean piece of linen, such as a handkerchief or a sheet. No coloured material should be used or the dye may get into the wound and cause blood poison.

Tear a long strip of the linen, about three or four inches wide. Roll it up in your fingers like a puttee, and starting below the wound, roll it round quite evenly, as if you were winding a puttee round your leg. Fasten it above the wound with a safety pin or slit the end of the bandage and tie the ends round the limb.

5. Sore feet.—Cleanliness is the best cure for sore feet. Keep your socks clean and darned. Before marching, rub your feet well with soap or oil, and see that your boots fit comfortably. Blisters should be pricked with a clean needle. Cover the part with a small bandage before putting on your sock. One is very liable to blood poison from scratches on the feet.

6. Sprains.—Dip a bandage in cold water and wrap it round the part affected. Keep the bandage wet.

7. Unless you are *absolutely certain* it is only a sprain and not a break or fracture of the bone, bind splints round the injured part before moving the patient.   This is most important.

8. Splints.—Splints must always be placed round a broken or fractured limb before the patient is moved. They can be made from anything that will not yield, such as wood, bayonets, rifles, etc.,   They should be padded with some soft material to prevent them hurting the injured limb.

9. Simple wounds.—Simple wounds should be well washed and bound in a clean bandage.

10. Bleeding.—If a man cuts or bursts an artery, namely, one of the larger veins in the body, he is in great danger of bleeding to death.   *Immediately* place your finger on the spot where the blood is spurting out and keep it pressed until medical aid can be obtained ;   or, wrap a penny or a small flat stone, in a piece of cloth and fix it in position with a bandage.   Place the patient in a lying position, and if the bleeding is from a leg or an arm raise the limb.

Should the bleeding still continue, tie a bandage tightly above the wound ;   by inserting a piece of stick and twisting it round, the required degree of tightness can be obtained.

11. Poison.—Ptomaine poison is found in decomposing food.

On active service when preserved meat and vegetables form a considerable proportion of the rations issued, soldiers are very liable to suffer from this form of poisoning.

12. The symptoms are violent pains in the stomach, vomiting and diarrhœa.

13. The best treatment is to induce the patient to continue vomiting until the stomach becomes empty. Then give him plenty of milk, if possible, boiled milk.

To induce vomiting give the patient a drink of water mixed with mustard.

Very little mustard will be necessary. If this is not available, open the mouth wide and tickle the throat with a feather, or make the patient press the first two fingers down his throat. The foregoing is the safest treatment in all cases of suspected poisoning.

14. Burns.—Apply oil or flour to the burnt part. Cut off the clothes, don't tear them away, and cover the wound quickly from the air.

15. Frostbite.—In case of frost bite, rub well the part affected with snow or cold water. Avoid taking the patient into a warm room until the part affected has gradually thawed.

16. A frost bite shows itself by a white patch on the skin. The danger is you may not know you have been bitten until too late, as you do not feel any pain at first.

In cold countries like Russia it is no uncommon thing for a complete stranger to rush up to you in the street and commence rubbing your nose with snow. He has noticed that your nose is being frost-bitten.

17. Drowning : rescue from.—Before attempting to rescue a drowning person, remove your boots and coat. They greatly impede your movements. Many a man has been drowned by the weight of his boots.

18. The Royal Life Saving Society recommend the following methods for rescuing a person from drowning.

(a) If the person does not struggle, turn him on his back, place your hands on either side of his head. Swim on your back with a steady kick of the legs, and husband your strength as much as possible.

Remember it is most important to keep the person's head above water.

(b) If he struggles, turn him on his back, catch his arms, just above the elbows, with a firm grip, draw his arms upwards at right angles and swim as before on your back.

(c) If he struggles violently, seize him under the arm or round the chest, and swim as before with a steady stroke on your back.

19. Rescuer's Wrists Seized.—" If the drowning person seizes hold of your wrists, turn both arms simultaneously against the drowning person's thumbs, outwards, and bring the arms in at right angles to the body. This will dislocate the thumbs of the drowning person if he does not let go. Then, as before, turn him on his back, and proceed to bring him to shore.

20. Rescuer Clutched Round the Neck.—" If clutched round the neck take a deep breath, lean well over the drowning person, immediately place one hand in the small of his back and pass the other over his face with the thumb and forefinger, pinching the nostrils close; at the same time

ace the palm of the hand on the chin and press away
ith all force possible.

21. Method of Assisting tired Swimmer.—"An easy
method of assisting a tired swimmer or one attacked by
cramp as well as others who might be quiet :—The person
assisted must place both hands on the shoulders of the
rescuer with the arms at full stretch and lie upon the
back. The rescuer being uppermost and having the arms
and legs free, swims with the breast stroke."

22. To restore animation.—Having got the drowning
person to land, there still remains the more difficult task
of restoring animation. Don't give stimulants, but send
immediately for medical aid, blankets and dry clothing.
If you are alone this will be impossible, as you cannot
leave the unconscious person. Shout for assistance.

23. Guiding principles.—The chief points to be remembered when restoring animation are :—
1. Restore the breathing.
2. Restore the circulation and heat of the body.
   If you restore the latter first, you will endanger
   the life of the patient.

24. To restore the breathing, loosen tight clothing,
especially the braces ; turn the patient face downwards,
clean away any matter such as weeds from the mouth
and nostrils, draw forward the tongue beyond the lips, and
secure it in that position by passing a strip of handkerchief
or piece of tape over the tongue and tying it under the
chin.

7

Turn the patient on his back, place a rolled coat or cushion under his shoulder blades.

Standing behind his head grasp his arms just above the elbows and draw his arms gently but steadily upwards above his head. Keep them stretched upwards for two seconds (This is to draw air into the lungs).

Now turn down the patient's arms and press them gently but firmly against the sides of his chest for two seconds (This is to press the air out of the lungs).

Repeat these movements regularly about fifteen times to a minute. Keep on repeating them for many hours until natural breathing is perceived, or a doctor has declared life extinct. If you have been able to send for blankets and dry clothing, the body may be dried and reclothed when they arrive, but this must not interfere with your efforts to restore the breathing.

25. To promote warmth.—When the patient has commenced to breathe naturally, promote warmth and circulation by rubbing the limbs upwards towards the heart (This will drive the blood towards the heart).

Cover the body with dry clothing, if this has not been already done, but keep on energetically rubbing the limbs through the clothing. Carry the patient to a house, put him to bed and apply heat (hot water bottles, hot bricks, etc.) to the soles of the feet, the arm pits, the pit of the stomach and between the thighs.

Give the patient plenty of fresh air.

26. To test if the powers to swallow have returned.—When life has been restored, test if the powers of swallowing have returned by giving the patient with a spoon a little warm water. If he succeeds in swallowing it, then give him in small quantities brandy and water, wine or coffee.

Encourage the patient to sleep.

27. Summary.—Put briefly, the points to be remembered are :—

1. Place the body face downwards, draw forward and secure the tongue. Send for medical aid, blankets and dry clothing.
2. Place the body on its back with a cushion under the shoulder blades. Immediately commence to restore breathing.
3. Restore warmth and circulation.

This treatment is known as Dr. Sylvester's method.

Questions on the Lecture

1. What would you do if a man fainted ?

2. If a man became unconscious from a fall on his head, or became ill after such a fall, how would you help him ?

3. What would you do in case of sunstroke ?

4. Describe how to make a bandage in case of emergency ?

5. How can you avoid sore feet ?

6. What would you do for a sprained ankle ?

7. How would you act if uncertain whether the injured limb was broken, fractured or only sprained ?

8. What are splints made of ?   How are they used ?

9. How would you treat a cut ?

10. Describe how you would prevent a man from bleeding to death ?

11. Why is a soldier specially liable to ptomaine poisoning ?

12. What are the symptoms of ptomaine poisoning ?

13. What is the best treatment for this and all cases of suspected poisoning ?

14. If a person fell into a fire, what would you do ?

15. How would you treat a frost-bite ?

16. How can you recognize a frost-bite ?

17. What should you do before attempting to rescue a drowning person ?

18. Describe three methods of bringing a drowning person to shore ?

19. How will you act if the drowning person seizes your wrists ?

20. If he clutches you round the neck, how will you get free ?

21. Describe an easy method of assisting a tired swimmer.

22. What would you do, having got the drowning person to land ?

23. Which would you restore first : the breathing, or the warmth and circulation of the body ?

24. Describe how you would restore the breathing.

25. How would you promote warmth and circulation ?

26. How would you test if the powers of swallowing had returned ?

27. Name briefly the points to be remembered when restoring animation ?

NOTE

SINCE the foregoing was written, and this little book went to press, startling events have occurred. So far as Ireland is concerned, the most remarkable is the never-to-be-forgotten declaration of Mr. John E. Redmond, the Irish leader, that the National Volunteers would join with their Ulster fellow-countrymen in the home defence, and that the Government were at liberty to withdraw the troops from Ireland. This has done more to unite us than all that has been said or done for a century. Ireland has been the Cordelia of the United Kingdom, and her spirit and generosity of character entirely misunderstood. All sections of the English people have to-day a true perception of Ireland's character, and England is as astonished as Lear when his wronged child came to his succour in his extremities :—

> " Mine eyes are not of the best
> But as I am a man I take this lady
> To be my child Cordelia."

" H."

Made in the USA
Monee, IL
16 September 2022

14048198R00057